A SONG FOR THE EARTH

A Song for the Earth

Shannon Jade

First edition 2025

Text and illustrations by Shannon Jade

ISBN (paperback) 978-1-7641436-0-8
ISBN (ebook) 978-1-7641436-1-5

Published by Wildflower Books

To Mum, who believes in this book – and in me.
Thank you for everything, every step of the way.

CITY

Home

The silver city towers high above me.
I crane my neck until I grow dizzy.

Home.
No, I am not at home.
Because I can't stay here,
where the city crumbles, crashing down.

A woman with an inky pen
and paper made from the trees
no longer standing
to cast these skyscraper shadows.

Home. I let it go.
I hear it rattle down the road
in a blaze of car horns
and beeping traffic lights.

I see the way this city suffers,
and so I quit turning another blind eye.

I cut loose these big-city shackles.
And hope for poems
that are more than words on paper
or the echo in my throat.

Soon, I swear it,
my simple words will spell
a song for the earth.

City Limits

I never recognised
the limits for what they were
until they boxed me in.
The whole world
S H R I N K I N G
to nothing more than the block
that surrounds apartment 224,
with its brassy number on the door
and the hinges that squeak in the night.

I keep trying to make myself fit this place,
like a square pretending to be a circle.
I keep trying to imagine
that my feet feel steady
where they strike the ground,
and my shoulders do not buckle
under the weight of all the things I do not say.

But lately, it isn't working.
Lately, everything is changing.
Of course I know why.

When the storms came,
they flooded us out of our homes.
Somewhere, the statue of liberty
is trapped and *sinking*.

When the fires burned,
they chased us from city streets,
to evacuation centre huddles,
where the hydrants were all out of water,
where we watched *ash* fall like *rain*.

I kept thinking the powers that be

would sit up, take notice,
and do something.
ANYTHING.
And they didn't let me down.

They signed new contracts
for gas and oil and fracking.
They thickened the lining of their wallets,
then drew the purse strings shut.

Beyond

I get the sense that the whole world
is greater than this place will ever let it be.

Hear whispers on the radio
when a *hurricane* tears up the coastline.
A stranger has lost everything.
Pockets empty of change.
No one will rebuild the ruins.

"You can't leave, January," my sister tells me.

Maybe she is right.
But I will never know
the miraculous truth of the earth itself
unless I find it running wild.

"Of course I can leave," I whisper. "I must."

Soon, I will follow the road less travelled
for as far as it will take me.
Watch the city's cleared spaces give way.

I think if I go, I might understand
why the city sinks and burns
and spirals like the wind,
and why its men in tailored suits
content themselves to sit back,
watching from high-up windows,
while they do nothing to help us at all.

Steely

"You are more of a follower
than a leader, January.
You are made to hear the cause
and never to speak it."
I remember my old report cards
and the guidance counsellors
who never thought I'd amount to much.

My resolve was always a delicate thing.
One good gust of wind,
and it might shatter into a thousand pieces.

I've never known who was right about me:
the world and its words
or my own, pressed to paper.

Today, I choose my words for myself.
I turn my resolve steely enough that even
the harshest storm will not be fit to break it.

Once, I might have listened.
And followed. And stayed.

But now, if I must,
    I will go.
        I will speak.
            I will lead.

My Last Coin

Instead of watching
the weather play out,
I work at keeping myself busy.

I put the apartment up for lease.
Tell my boss to give away my desk
at the office job that will not miss me
past a talent for mapping out spreadsheets
and hunting to find the right answers.

I spend my last coin on better gumboots.
And this journal full of crisp blank pages.

Because I seek the truth
that the tabloids won't tell us.
C H A N C E S
before they're all gone.

The whole world is waiting
for someone to find it.
And why shouldn't that someone be me?

The Wild

"You're wild,"
my colleagues tell me
when I say I will leave
the city behind me.

I never say much,
only smile and nod
and pack my bags
before boarding
the next train
and plane
and car
to wherever
I am headed.

"You're wild,"
my friends call out
as they wave me goodbye.

"Yes. Exactly.
We all are at least
a little bit wild.
Don't you think?
Yes, I am wild,
so I am going
to find my wilderness,"
I wish I would reply.

Instead, I seal my lips.
I smile politely
and offer
one last wave.

Then I turn

and do not look back
to find the button-up coats
or the shiny silver skyscrapers
shedding a tear
as they
     watch
          me
              go.

Grey Skies Blue

Sometimes,
the sweeping city skies
are hard to tell apart
from the metallic grey tones
of the buildings just ahead.

Somewhere,
the *smoke* and *smog*
disappear
and make way
for *clear blue skies*
it's hard to believe we share.

As I leave the city
in my murky dust,
I watch it fade,
my head resting
against the train window.

I do not look for the changing shapes
of the land that speeds away.

Instead, I watch the skies
and count the clouds until
a *deep and dark* gradient of grey
fades and turns *fresh blue.*

Speed Away

I watch the city speed away,
and I think the greatest artists
are those who aren't afraid to roam.

It's easiest to write the world
when you've got to know it well.

All my life, I might wonder
what anything is for.

And so I quit waiting
for answers
without wings
enough to find me.

I find the way I don't know yet.
I leave behind the not knowing.

The city made of flashing lights.
The phone screen always bright,
glowing in the palm of my hand.

I speed towards the quiet places,
with room enough for growing bored
and time enough for finding out
what it really means to be *alive*.

I set out to find an adventure,
and I hope to find much more.

RAINFOREST

Meeting the Forest

I meet the forest like a sun shower
finding the puddles left by the storm.
I get to know the humid air,
stinging where it strikes the skin.

At first, I see the shades of green,
but the forest has a slow way
of introducing itself to strangers.
Time offers glimpses of reds and blues,
pinks and oranges, violets and glowing golden tones.

I meet the forest like I am finding my feet.
Climbing, always climbing.
I get to know it little by little,
never moving so suddenly
as to scare it away.
When I am patient,
there is plenty to notice.
Sounds that only exist here,
in the quiet spaces.
The smell of *petrichor*
that waltzes permanently
through the air as I breathe it.

I meet the forest, and I like who I meet.
I am quiet and gentle, and I am hopeful
that, with a little time,
the forest will learn
to like me too.

I See Starlight

I used to complain
on nights when I couldn't sleep
because the days were long
or the sirens too loud.
But I no longer seem to worry.

On nights when my eyes won't shut,
it is because the world is so quiet.
I hear poetry *echo* all around me,
and I scratch out the words I can remember
by the pitiful light of the *stars*.

In the city, there were always
too many streetlamps to see starlight.
Here, stars are always crowded out
by the leaves and branches
that vie for attention up above.

Still, I do not let the darkness bother me.

On nights when sleep will not find me,
I reach a hand
                    up, up, up.

I stretch it out ahead of me,
like I am grasping for starlight
to hold it in the palm of my hand.

I cannot make out the outlines of my fingers.
I am much too small for reaching the sky.

But if at night, I see a falling star,
a small piece of me believes that together...
the forest and me might just *catch it.*

The Lakes

If the skies are for the birds,
then the lakes are for the poets.
I have always believed this,
and I find the truth of it now.
The trees kiss the surface of the water,
and it is hard to separate
reality from its reflection.
And though I have long since dreamed
I might sit by the lakes
and write one great soliloquy
they could print next to my name
in the history books...

The lakes are not the story.

I walk on careful tiptoe
and draw close enough
to find my mirror staring back at me.
It is not alone.

There is a man around my own age,
with broad shoulders and sharp cheekbones
and eyes the same striking green as the forest itself.
I see him, and my breath catches.
For a poet, I seem to run awfully short on words.

My attention snags like fabric on branches.
And I cannot tear it back to my one great soliloquy
or the lakes that ought to have made it true.

Caio and Maria

"Caio."
He tells me his name through the weight of a heavy accent.
"And this is Maria."
She and her long, dark hair appear from the trees.
"January," I reply.

My voice is never loud enough
to rustle the leaves.
Perhaps they ask me who I am
or why I am here.
I don't remember exactly.
But I know that I tell them
about the office buildings stretching higher
than all the rainforest's trees,
the tinny helicopters that could give
the birds a run for their money.

"I am here," I say, "to find the world again
because I am not sure it exists anymore
in that place made up of so much concrete."

Neither Caio nor Maria answer me.
She nods sharply, while he offers a smile
that might be reassuring or sceptical.
Or both in equal parts.

Caio and Maria, who make me the promise
that I'll know the forest like it's my own.
I follow them into the undergrowth.

Dinner

By dinner time, I find company.
"Join us," Caio and Maria tell me.
"Our family will want to meet you.
To teach you how to climb."
I find it hard to believe.
I agree anyhow.

Dinner used to be
a quiet affair,
a tray table balancing
leftovers on my knee.

In a world where nothing had changed.

Instead, I feel barely hungry.
I gather around a dirt floor table
and am offered more than my share.

"You live here, in the forest?"
I ask over delicate scraps and morsels.

An older woman smiles.
"It looks like you do too."

The Forest Today

"The forest is changing, now more than ever."
The woman insists I call her Grandmama.
She explains that nothing is as simple
as always staying just the same.
"It never was an easy place to live," she says.
I believe her by her words and the scars on her skin.
"But now it faces challenges unlike before."
She looks to the trees, high up above.
"Less life. More danger. Trying times ahead."

I notice the cadence of her voice,
how she points to the trees nearest,
as if she could call each one by its name.

"Why?" I ask, my words just a whisper.
"What makes the forest change now?"
I glance over and find Maria,
no longer laughing but watching the woman,
waiting—I realise—for her answer.

"Time," Grandmama says simply.
"And people," she tells me.
An uncommon look passes across her face,
halfway to sadness, swaying to an apology.
"Of course, that's not to mention
all the changing that starts
with the money rolling around your city,
and the way everyone always needs *more*."

Danger

The forest
seems grand
and unshakeable,
yet Maria tells me
it is much too fragile.
"This whole world
is a threat to the rainforest."
Why? I wonder
before I ask it.

Soon, I learn about the trees
that fall...
      ...fall...
           ...fall...
for factories
    and farming space
        and for fires that ravage the land.

Soon, I learn about the air
that is warmer now than it used to be
and the landscape changing fast
from green to *gold* and *grey*.

"Why won't anyone do something?" I whisper.
Maria smiles a little sadly and asks me,
"What will ever be enough?"

Rain Falling

Every year, rain falls and drenches the forest
thousands of millimetres deep.
Up to 50 percent of the forest's rain
belongs to the trees that recycle water and bring it home.[1]
Here, it rains not in that sporadic way
of drizzle on the M5 motorway
but most of the time, 200 days in every 365.[2]
When it isn't pouring, the mist is enough
to leave the air too damp for my cityscape lungs.
Still, I know that raining often is not enough.
Here, the trees that die give up on building weather
and herald droughts that cull their brothers and sisters.

"Hot air holds more damp than the cool can," Maria explains.
        "We will brave the drought, and someday,
                we will face the flood."

Faster, I watch us speed towards a *tipping point*,
when sweeping greens will fade to dusty gold.
Or when the rain will only fall in sheets
that transform the forest into a sea.

Every year, rain falls and drenches the forest
thousands of millimetres deep.[3]
But as the forest becomes someplace new,
no one here ever is certain
whether this year's rainfall
will be *enough* or far *too much.*

Listening for Birdsong

According to Caio,
the birds are changing
every bit as much as the trees.
"They finished a study
not so long ago," he says.
"The scientists found
birds that were smaller
with wings that stretched wider
than they used to."[4]

I am silent for a moment.
"The birds are changing?"
I ask when I'm able.
"But what use is changing weight or wings?"

Caio stares up at the sky,
where the birds soar
in fewer numbers than expected.
"The smaller they are,
the less energy they need.
And in the end?" Caio says.
"The birds are like us.
We all are just trying
to survive the hotter air
and the unpredictable rains
and the worry for every next meal."

Savannah

Fire and drought
are growing too heavy
for the forest
to carry on holding.
Soon, 75 percent
of this rich green world
could turn to the dry
and arid dust
of a savannah.[5]
A savannah!

Here, in what always
ought to have been
a rainforest,
teaming with *life* and *colour*.

A savannah,
where the birds
lack trees for perching,
where the skies
rarely relinquish
any fresh rain.

A savannah.
It's hard to believe.
But sometimes,
when I close my eyes,
I swear I can already
feel the transition begin.

In the Treetops

I run. I jump. I climb.
Higher, higher still.
I know the forest best
when I look down upon it
from my place among the clouds.
Every day, I discover
another little piece of the rainforest.

Did you know that the tallest trees
reach 290 feet skywards
and almost towards the heavens?[6]
Or that there are 80,000
different types of plants
all living in the forest with me?[7]
I didn't. I didn't know.
But now? Now I am learning.

The forest is home to intelligent birds
that live well into their sixties.
And sometimes, it feels quiet,
but I am one of more than 30 million people
who call the forest a home too.[8]

Wilder. Wilder. Wilder.
In a place like this, there is always
so much more to discover and to hope for.
I race to the treetops on what I think
is probably a Tuesday, and I climb
until I run out of world for reaching.

Sometimes, I think I must have arrived
in the rainforest with my eyes shut.
At first, I only saw face value
of the tall trees and their leaning shadows.
Over time, I have learned to look. To listen too.

"I'm searching for clearings," I say, and I find them,
like footprints carving hollows in sand
in all the places they do not belong.
The land is too many spaces
where ash gathers but trees never do,
where the forest gives way and *burns out*.

Not Quite Thunder

The sound of thunder
is low and echoing
long before the storm.
The forest is quieter
and drier and stiller
than it should be.
I am only waiting.
A strange sense of foreboding
hangs aloft, waiting too.

Thunder clouds are mounting pressure,
and I feel it like weight pressing heavy on my chest.

Breathe. Slowly.
The first clap of thunder
B O O M S.

I shut my eyes and imagine
lightning flashes a searing gash in the sky.
I have never minded the weather,
even on the city's dreariest days.

So perhaps I wouldn't mind
the wild of a fresh storm
if what I heard truly was
the sound of thunder
and not the heavy weight
of trees made for climbing
instead of striking solid ground.

Racing

I climb down from treetops
and take charge.

Footsteps *strike*
a steady beat
as I race
F A S T
to the clearings.

I run with the wind
until my breath burns
at the bottom of my lungs.
I race until there's no more space
left for running.
Until the trees begin to thin
and give way
to someplace
hollow.

Men and Machines

I stumble upon a clearing,
a place where fallen trees
make way for an expanse of empty space,
where the leaves do not lean
to cover the sky,
where the chill of the wind
has nothing to stand in its way.

I stop still.
Quiet.
Waiting.

Beside me, I hear
Maria draw in a sharp breath
that whistles through her bared teeth.
"It's another deforestation project," she hisses,
voice harsher than I've heard it before.

Caio points to the men and their machines
that line the edges of the receding tree line.
"Better for pockets full of cash
and worse for the wealth of the forest."

I feel as though I am watching a movie,
a sum of plot points I can't appreciate.
It's a train wreck speeding forward,
and I can't look away.

Like a Forest Fire

Fury burns in me
like the early sparks
of a forest fire,
    embers soaring
        up in the air
            and twisting
                with tendrils of smoke.

I watch the forest *wither*.
The branches snap and break.
The sky clouds over, and soils sink low,
and dense trees turn to clearings.

I have known anger,
when my little sister stole my dolls
or when the school's biggest bully
wouldn't let me sit with the rest of the group for lunch.
Now the anger climbs higher.
It rises like the *summer sun*,
until it is bigger than I am.

Fury *burns* brighter than the fires
that would turn the rainforest
to nothing more than dust.
"Why isn't anyone helping?" I demand to know.
"Where are the helpers?" I ask.

They aren't here. There is only us. All alone.
And we are the forest's only hope.

Clouds of Dust

The forest loses power
as trees fall to the ground
in thick clouds of dust.
My time here has taught me
how little it takes to make a big impact.

For better or for worse.

On its own, this might not be quite such a disaster.
It might not steal away so much of the forest
as to keep the earth from blooming and healing.
It might not matter so much that machines
with their sharp, jagged angles
work to turn the wild urban,
the forest into someplace I might find
a graffiti-covered train station wall.

But these mining, farming clearings
are scattered all throughout the rainforest,
with more appearing each and every day.
The big-city billionaires can never earn enough
without wanting an extra dollar.
They don't care about the damages.
These are the damning damages
no one minds while they are lucrative.

My anger sparks like a flare. I hear my own voice roaring
as loud as these T I G E R S made of metal parts.

Money Matters

Money matters, I know.
Some days, I think it matters alone.
Certainly, it might to the fancy business people
with suits and ties and freshly shined shoes.

Money matters when it pays to make itself,
when it funds the next great technological innovation
designed to tear trees down or pull oil up.

It is a difficult thing to learn that no one
from the city must care very much
about the forest or its people.
All until they care about
the thin plastic cards
maxed out to their limits
and the way the forest might earn them back
just a little extra cash they can spend.

There's nothing we can do. Not really.
And who will listen to a voice as quiet as mine?

Money matters more, more, more.
To the men and women in their fancy business suits
and to the lowly paid workers they lord it over.

Money matters. Of course it does.
But I wish the earth mattered *more*.

For the Future

"What do you think is next?" I ask.
"For the forest?" says Maria.
She stops for a moment
to think of an answer.
"The thinning of the trees,"
she tells me, looking sorry.
"Soils that turn to dust
instead of to mud.
Too many of us
scrambling for food
and whatever room
is left among the trees."

I hold my breath
and count to three.
"Isn't there something,
anything we can do?" I ask.

Maria shrugs her shoulders.
"Maybe," she concedes.

Hope flutters in my chest.

Then Maria continues.
"But time is running out," she says.
"And we're all running low on ideas."

If a Tree Falls in the Forest

Even in my short time here,
I'm certain I notice a shift.

The air gets *heavier*
a little at a time
until it weighs me down.

The birdsong *fades*
to an echoing quiet,
eerie in the early morning.

It is hard to believe
that no one worries for
the kind of danger
and devastation
we know is coming,
just not when.

I hear my voice
an octave too high
as I give up wondering
the sound a forest makes
when it all falls apart.

It's hard to say whether anyone minds.

"If a tree falls in the forest,
is anybody listening at all?"

The Miners

With all my fury,
I cannot sit still.
I go to the clearings,
where the miners gather
with the machines
that tear us all down.

"Do something," I tell them.
"It's your world too,
and you're breaking it down.
Won't you wake up
before it's too late?"

I hear my voice as if it is someone else's,
a red raw sting in my throat.

The miners watch me
with tired, blinking eyes
until my anger burns out
and goes up in smoke.

Are you listening?
I wonder, when I know they aren't.

But just for a moment,
these people look
every bit as nervous,
as worn out and fried,
as the forest and I do too.

My tears fall like the rain that won't.

I move with steps that thunder
until I disappear among the trees.

In the quiet of the forest,

before I make it back to camp,
I cry my eyes out for the cloudy skies
and the canopies of leaves
I'm not sure I can rescue.

Then I climb for as far
as the last trees will take me.
Let the forest look small,
like a problem I can solve.

A Bright Idea

A bright idea finds me late in the evening,
with the strength of a thing with wings,
under the dim glow of last light,
when I am least expecting it.
I recognise it like I'd know the stars
and the constellations
that stretch all the way home.

I am quiet at dinner,
giving my food away
to someone who looks hungrier
and answering questions
with only gentle smiles
and quiet nods of my head.

All the while, I feel my fingers itching
to drown themselves in ink
and commit a bright idea
to paper and to memory
so that maybe...
Just maybe...

There is something,
something valuable,
that I can do
to make a *difference*.

Until It Shatters

I rarely know what to do or how to help.
My words are weapons put to paper.

Here among the treetops,
I wonder where to turn,
and then I remember:
time is always marching on.
If I look very carefully,
I swear the forest
has carved a map
of footprints I could follow.

One step at a time,
I gather up truths.
Dug up from the earth.
Retrieved from the lakes.
Captured from the skies.

I search for power and impact and honesty
hidden among the forest greens.

It is never enough simply to write a poem
or to scream it loud into the void.
It is never enough, in this forest falling down.
But it is *something*.

My voice may be too fragile
not to break, but I promise
to shout and sing until it *shatters*.

Pressed Leaves and Poetry

I swear I find patterns
stitched into everything
that keeps the forest alive.

I know this place like a list of facts
I might memorise before a pop quiz.
The rainforest is home to 10 percent of all Earth's species.[9]
The forest is home to almost 400 billion trees,
drinking up the rain, then releasing it back into the atmosphere.[10]

As time has gone on, my clever book smarts
have made way for tangible truths.
I know how to taste a storm
before the first clap of thunder.
I learn how to tell the time
by the light of the sun
and the call of the birds
instead of the hands on my watch.

The secret forest is a mystical place
I'm not sure I quite believe in.
Just when I think I might be nearly an expert,
a new mystery reveals itself
to remind me how little I know.
And now that I must leave so soon,
I am certain only of uncertainty,
that I cannot know all I wish I would.

Late at night, I record my facts in looping cursive
and press leaves to paper to dry.
All the while, I wish on the stars
that I will know the forest
at least well enough to spare it.

Building Histories

Then we are building history.
Or at least, we're watching
while someone else does,
towers stacking higher
while the tree stumps go low.

The landscape changes quickly,
and it doesn't take long before
some spaces are difficult to recognise.
We are the casualties that go unnoticed,
the battlers who fall victim
to the land-clearing machines
and never make a newspaper's headline.

The elders teach me the sweeping history
of the forest that has always been their home.
"Deforestation is not new, January.
We will simply have to do our best
with the new piece of history we are given."

I nod politely and listen to their words.
But the truth they offer does not seem very fair.

Why are we letting the city build histories
for a place it can never understand?

"We've always been running," says Caio.
"Maybe it's time to start standing our ground."

"Damn right," Maria tells me,
and she claps a hand down on my shoulder.
"It's high time we do something better than flee.
It's high time we had our own say
in this history that's walking all over us."

Into the Night

Into the night,
I reach for the clouds.
I balance my notebook
on the edge of my knee.

I look up to find
the gaps in the trees
and glimpse traces of starlight
shining through like diamonds,
S P A R K L I N G.
I think I find galaxies
swirling circles high above.

My poems do not bury me.

Instead, I climb them,
one gentle step at a time,
reaching my hands
so that one day, I might
run my fingers through the clouds.

This universe is grand enough to frighten me.

In the gentle quiet of the forest sleeping,
I rarely close my eyes.
Instead, I drag my hand across the pages
and give up all my best words to the skies.

Something More

I realise with a start
that I do not know
how long it has been
since I left the city.
Weeks, maybe?
Months?

Something more
waits out there
for me and my book of poems.
I make my plans to turn my back and walk away
from someplace I could have stayed.

For all of the missing I will feel
for this land among the trees,
I know that it is time
to close a well-read chapter
in favour of finishing the book.

Before the Dawn

I wake in the early hours,
when the sky still believes it is night.
Ink patterns stain my face
where I have fallen asleep
with pen and paper held close.
I stand and stretch
while I wait for the sunrise.

Finally, small fractals of light
break glittering lines through the treetops,
the air itself seeming to shimmer
like the surface of those great poet's lakes.

A car rumbles in the distance,
and I know it is here for me.
So I return to the soils
and tidy my makeshift camp
until it looks as good as new.

I turn on my heel, and I march
away from the forest and its gifts.
I take nothing with me,
except for my poems and my hope
built from pieces of the land.

A Song for the Forest

At first, I feel foolish, the baby bird
ready to launch from its nest
with wings still unsure how to fly.

I watch the sky fade
from blue and silver clouds
to shades of pink and gold
before it dims to midnight dark.
Just one more time,
I count the last
of the fading constellations
I find up above
and imagine I see a wishing star.

For just one more night,
I am a city girl turned forest wild
with mud in my hair and a spirit running riot.

In the light too faint to see by,
I etch my words onto paper pages.
And I promise with all the truth I have to give...

I will write a song for the forest.

DESERT

The Desert Sun

The desert sun
glows golden
  as it reaches
  the earth,
      which rises
      and falls
          in sloping,
          sandy dunes.
              The air seems
              to *shimmer*, like
              the light is too
              bright
          for the usual spectrum
          of colours
          that give way
      to yellow,
      orange,
      rust.
  The harsh of
  the desert
  calls out to me
with open arms
that welcome me
home.

Tipping Points

The locals set up camp
and tell me to call it my home.
Even when I know we won't stay long.
Canvas tents sit light in the sand
with a perfect view of the sky's stars.

"Have you travelled a long way?"
a man with kind eyes, Ahmed, asks me.
I tell him I have travelled far enough
and yet never enough, no, not ever.

A girl smiles at me from across the camp.
"Imani," she introduces herself. "And my sister, Ade."

I tell them my name is January,
that I plan to know the world
beyond the half-truths
of the city that raised me.
There is so much to discover, I say,
in this place that is so unlike home,
a place that I hear is already speeding
towards the tipping points set
to send it roaring over the edge.

"You will know the desert
soon enough," Imani promises,
as if it is not under any threat.
"And so long as you respect her,"
she tells me lightly, "the desert will treat you well."

After Sundown

This travelling caravan
and our heavy footsteps,
stepping stones along the sands.

The days are coolest
when they give way to night,
when the sun sinks low
and out of sight.

After sundown,
the desert's people
fall asleep, one by one.
Often, I am tired
by the burdens
of a day in the bright.

Still, I believe in the power of a poem.
And I remember why I am here.

So every night,
by the light of the moon
and the stars,
I hold my pen in my fist,
and I scratch my words
down on paper
until at last,
I fall
asl——————

As Far as the Eye Can See

Sometimes, I wake in the middle of the night,
and perhaps, I miss the forest.
The desert falls an eerie quiet
with no gentle breeze
or soaring birds
to break it.
The sand reaches towards
a distant horizon
so that I know just how easy
it would be to get lost.

Never am I sure of my place in this world.
The smallest trace of panic settles in my chest.

Just when I think
I am all out of courage,
the faintest *sunbeam*
climbs free
from the darkness.

I sit alone
and watch
as the cool night
falls to pieces
and clears space
for the rich, glowing hope
of another sunny day.

Far From City Lights

The heat of the desert
is harsher for being dry.
There is no humidity
in the stony air,
which lets the sunrays
through to burn.
So often, the desert days
are unbearably hot,
only for the night
to bring a chill
that settles in my bones.

Sunlight scolds across my shoulders.
Heat carves cracks in my skin.

Yet for as much
as the desert
tries to break me,
I cannot help
but find its beauty.
In the dazzling light
of gold, glowing sunbeams
that roll right out of sight.
For the patterns of stars
that all tell stories
unlike any
I ever found
drenched in city lights.

How to Survive

Slowly, I learn to survive.
Marching always onwards.

How to stay cooler
by covering my skin
and avoiding the peak
of afternoon sunlight.
How to cook couscous
and make the meal stretch
when there's barely
enough for us all.
Where to find shelter
and where to find food.
Where to find the day
through the dark of the night.

More than they teach me
the tools for surviving,
the people of the desert
offer lessons I'll keep
that remind me
what surviving is good for.

The reasons we fight through the hard days
only to call them our happy memories.

Sunburning

My skin is soon enough sunburned
by the sting of the searing sun.
I turn to shades of red, then bronze,
freckles like paint spills
across the bridge of my nose.
Sand burns hot under my feet.
Sunbeams flare and fracture
with a heat of such force
that I can see the air climb,
like shimmery waves
rising back up
towards the sky.

The light turns in
and reflects back on itself
until it is a mirage
that makes everything
look just like a dream,
so that I am never sure
of what I am seeing.

The desert itself?
        Or the picture it paints.

Fire and Famine

Another drought has seized control
and holds the desert in its fiery grip.
"What does it mean?"
I ask the people who'd know.

"It means we cannot trust
if or when the rains will fall,"
they tell me sharply.
"There's no telling how long
the water we have will have to last."

I learn that the desert is growing,
eight percent from 1950 up until 2015.[11]

The warming world gives way to spaces
this hot and dry and sandy.
The expanding desert lands
claim new places, a little at a time,
where the rains will not fall,
where crops just will not grow.
And what next? What then?
I wonder but do not ask.
No one offers up answers
to the questions that won't touch my lips.

But here in the silence,
I think we all know that someday,
the rains will be too late.

Water's Worth

Water brought the wars
        when there never was enough.

Once, Ahmed says, this land ran with water,
back when it was home
to people who left drawings
to age on stony cave walls.
Now, it hardly ever rains.
In some places, the clouds only give up
a mere three inches of water a year.[12]

Here, in the heart of the desert,
something to drink is worth fighting for.
For hundreds of thousands of far-reaching miles,
tensions rise to boil when the water and wells run dry.

I never drink too fast.

I cup the precious little water
in the palms of my hands,
and I drink it just like *gold*
that might as soon disappear.

For every ounce
        of wartime water,
                I turn it into wishes.

I wish for no more battles. I wish for winter rains.
I wish for wishing water before the desert dies of thirst.

Oasis

Some days, I think
I have entered a state
of delirious hope.

I have read a million stories
about the dusty, dry deserts
and the faint flicker of light
that looked like blue and green.
Before, I always believed
that the idea of oasis
was a fallacy, really.
Who could find sanctuary
in a place where it didn't exist?
Now I know different and better.

Sometimes, around midday,
the sun reaches its highest point
in the clear, cloudless sky.
I stare off into the distance,
fix my gaze somewhere
far off and up ahead.

And if I squint my eyes,
tilt my head just to the right,
I swear I see a splash of colour
break up brown, red, and gold.

"Oasis," I whisper then,
          as I find it in the waves
                    of the rising desert heat.

The waterless places reach further afield,
and we have to trek a longer distance
to find enough for all of us to drink.

My eyes are playing tricks on me now,

when I look skywards
and think I see clouds
that promise me fresh rain will fall.

Even when it burns me,
like fire and smoke,
I try not to keep noticing the heat.

I kneel in the sands
and cup my hands together.
I am certain that water pools
in the wrinkles of my skin.
But always, when I stand
and feel the droplets
trickle back to the ground,
I am disappointed again
to find that it is only
falling sand,
like an hourglass
      running
          out of time.

Heatwaves and Sandstorms

Today, as we travel,
the heatwave joins forces
with the violence of a sandstorm.

Experts believe that winds pick up
about 100 million tons of dust
and debris from the desert every year.[13]

Imani tells me she knows because
of a book she once read about home.
"What this means," she says,
"is that the wicked sandstorms
clog the air with dirt and dust."

I feel the winds whip fiercely
in twisting and turning spirals.
Rough, gritty sand sinks low
to the bottom of my lungs,
and I cannot cough it loose.

"The storms can travel
over far, great distances,"
Imani tells me earnestly.
"Even as far as America.
Or the rich, green Amazon."

Huh. I hear my voice as just a hum.

I catch the sandy particles
so they run through my fingers
before the wind carries them off.
I wonder how much of this far-away desert
will find its way to Caio and Maria
and the rainforest I left behind.

Threat

All the while,
I always remember
the dangers that threaten
the future of here.
The desert and
the people who live here,
the far-reaching land
and the way that it all
could disappear
in less than a lifetime.

Gone up in a blaze and then nothing but *ash*.

As much as I try
and wrack my brains,
I cannot fathom
why no one
from the great, towering city
is doing anything
to keep this place safe.

Anthropogenic

Most of the damage is anthropogenic.
It's people who are always to blame.

"It comes from your cities," says Ade,
while Imani glances up at me,
looking almost apologetic.
"It comes from the tall buildings
that churn through electricity
and from cars that set smog
loose to choke the atmosphere."

I know it is true, and the truth sends
my hands curling up to make fists.

The desert is at risk, under threat,
not because it has to be.
Not because it was destiny.
But because a few suited workers
with their city view offices
won't quit drilling for oil
until it runs dry.

Because the people with power
are so good at planning
to be richer tomorrow,
that most have forgotten
we still need a world that lasts us well
when we quit *counting days*
to *chase the years* instead.

Call for Aid

"Why is there no help?"
I ask when night falls cool again.
Where are the helpers?
I want to know.

The governments and aid organisations
that could offer food and water and peace.

"The government lacks the resources
to offer the help we need.
The aid from overseas can only do so much,"
Ahmed replies patiently.

"And besides," he says.
"What use is calling for aid
when the problem is here at home?
What we need is not help
but a solution," he says.
"That eases the sandstorms
and brings new rains
and stops the heat from climbing."

It strikes me then
that what the desert needs
might be a call for aid
that gives up supporting
whatever hurts it more.

Fire

I am small, and the desert large.
The problem is bigger
than the solving words
I keep in my throat.

And still, there is fire
here in my heart,
the kind that sets
a landscape ablaze.

Anger grows as I think
of the system
that strips the desert
for all it is worth
to fuel consumption
that makes this place
worth less...
       and less...
              and less.

I look around
for someone to blame,
but all I can find
is my own afternoon shadow.

My anger searches the dunes
and finds no place to land.

Mission for Truth

I fight my way
across the desert,
and I embark
on a mission for truth
that takes me to
the limits.

Everywhere
I turn to look,
I see the cracks
of desert crumbling.
I cannot help
but think of *kintsugi*,
the Japanese art
of piecing
broken pieces
back together,
mending cracks
with *gold*.

For all the ways
the desert is broken,
it is beautiful too.
The desert deserves
the honesty that might
just have power
for saving it.

Time Gone By

By the light of so many stars,
I often write my poems
late into the night
or the early morning.

A page at a time,
I draw a map that reaches
not from here to there
but from then to now.
I sort back through
my own stories
and look for where
everything went wrong.

I find the desert is death by a thousand small cuts.

So I give up on history
and search for how
to turn time gone by
into a revival
for the years
still left to come.

Uncertain

"I am not so sure,"
Ahmed tells me
when I say it is time
to make a change.

"Who are we?" he asks.
"To disrupt the status quo?"

I understand those who wait
for the desert to right itself,
still believing in their years
of time spend here in the sands
and the way things used to be.

"I am afraid," I argue calmly,
"that not being sure is a luxury.
That if someone isn't sure
enough to act very soon,
then for everyone,
it will wind up too late."

Worse, Still

Worse, still, conditions become,
even when I think it's not possible.
Worse, still, the soils dry up.
The hunger strikes rumbling like
the thunder that won't clap.
Worse, still, anxieties collide,
falling and floundering
to a cacophony of noise.
Worse, still, I start to wonder
just how much time
is left on the clock
before the seconds tick down
and all the time in the world
to make things better, still,
speeds towards midnight
and at last runs out
altogether.

Critical

"Okay. It is time."
Ahmed and some other elders
greet me in the early hours
of a crisp, clear desert morning.

I wipe the sleep from my eyes.
"It's time?" I ask, confusion
lacing the current of my voice.

The people who know the desert best
gesture to the space all around them,
as if to say that it speaks for itself.

I watch the sands kick up another storm
that tints the air the colour of rust.
I feel the heat climb across my skin,
even though the sun has barely risen.

"It is time," a woman repeats gently.
She points to the old journal
that I use as a pillow on nights
when I don't fall asleep still writing.
"It's critical to try for a difference,"
she says, her words printed
in the lines of her face.
"Before, as you say, the time is gone.
Let us act now, while there still is a chance."

Never Give Up

"I really think you could make a difference,"
Imani and Ade say brightly,
somewhere from out of the blue.

"I'm not sure what do, exactly,"
I tell them honestly. "I'm not sure
that I know anything at all."

To my surprise, Imani smiles.
"You're never too confident.
Because you know it matters.
You're in this not for fame or money."

Ade turns to me, with sharp eyes
that mirror my own face back at me.
"I think you could help us,
and I hope that you will.
Can you promise to never give up?"

When she says it just so,
there are no questions left over.
So I give her my word, my voice unshaking.

"No quitters," I whisper, out here in the desert.
"I can't promise anything except not to cave."

I won't.

Rising from the Sands

So I rise from the sands
with my head held high
and watch my shadow
tower tall and reach
across the dunes.

I feel the beat of a purpose
strike a steady rhythm.

I set my jaw and fix my gaze
and stretch my arms towards the sun.

As if I'm climbing skywards,
always chasing higher ground.

I stand upon the sand dunes
in the early morning and late at night.
With all of the power I can muster up,
I call out my words so the sun can hear me.

I let my voice ride
the waves of rising heat
all the way to cloudless skies.

I tell stories we all can believe in,
in hopes that someone will listen and act.

Fast. And fierce. And still fighting.

Sketching

Fierce and angry,
I return now
to sketching poems,
angled words
carved on paper
until I find
the right ones.

The desert burns
all around me,
and for right now,
it is all I can do
to shout out for help,
to lend my voice
just as furious
as the flames.

Through the Sandstorms

The sandstorms take hold
and drown the desert
in its own layers
so that I barely
can see a distance
just a metre ahead of me.

Even as the dunes
disintegrate,
as the pieces fly
through the air
around me,
I do not bow
my head and cower.

I stand tall
and march strong,
like a warrior
riling to wage
another war.

One Last Goodbye

I know I cannot stay here
any more than I could
at the heart of the forest.

I chase the desert closer to its other side
and prepare to watch it fall far behind me.

"I knew you'd have to leave,"
Imani says when I tell her
it's time for me to go.
"You'll be careful," Ade warns.
"You'll do good," Ahmed demands.

I hold their words like prayers.
I keep my promises true.

When it comes to choices, to stay or to go,
I know I have little say in the path that I claim.
The desert leads the way,
and I am a fool if I do not follow.

"One day, we'll meet again,"
I say until I believe it.
I wave one last goodbye,
the movement seeming to produce an echo
that collides with space all around me.

The sound of leaving is low and melancholy.
A song when I can't catch the tune.

A Song for the Desert

A little at a time,
the rolling, sweeping sands
fade off into the distance.

A little at a time,
the epic scale of the dunes
gives way to only distant hills
that might be made of sand.

I watch the desert
slip from my grasp
until I cannot see it anymore.

I whisper my promises
so that I can still hear them.
"I will write you a poem,"
I tell whoever is listening.
"I promise, a song for the desert."

OCEAN

The Edge of the Ocean

I reach the edge of the ocean,
and I listen for the waves
as they crash to shore.
I smell the tangy salt
twisting through the air.
I feel the cool water
wash away the sand
and desert heat.
I close my eyes,
and I stand very still.
For a moment,
I do not ask
anything of myself
or of the world.
As soon as I find the ocean,
I listen for the waves
rolling out to sea.

The Shallows

A step a time, I wade into the shallows
so that the salty sea water brushes my ankles.

Sharp-edged seashells
line the ocean floor.
Shimmering colours
turning bright,
I R I D E S C E N T
as they reach through the surface
to catch the sunlight.

The boat is an old vessel,
with faded lettering to barely spell
what once must have been a name.
A sail billows violently in the wind
yet shows no signs it will snag or tear.

My land-locked legs wobble
just slightly beneath me
as I step on board the boat
and the choppy waves
that keep it afloat.

Another wave and an easier goodbye.
A moment later, we are setting sail.

At the End of the World

Just before nightfall,
the other passengers and me
gather at the edge of the boat.
We lean over a balcony
and wait to watch the sunset.

If it weren't for the company,
I think I would fear
I had found the end of the world.

The sky turns to shades
of dazzling pink
and orange and lilac
before it fades
to navy blue.

And when the sun is gone,
I realise there is nothing at all.
Only the faint shimmer of *moonlight*
striking the waves for a moment
before they roll and crash
to the bottom of the ocean again.

"Incredible, isn't it?"a woman mutters.
I think she means to speak to herself.
But I find an answer anyway.
"Incredible," I whisper.

And maybe just a little bit terrifying.

Like a Lullaby

I do not expect
    for sleep to come easy,
        but it turns out,
    I am tireder
than I realised.
    Like a cradle,
        the gentle rocking
    of the boat
puts me to sleep
    as the crashing waves
        stay always in rhythm,
    never missing a beat,
like a lullaby
    that knows all the words.
        When at last,
    my eyes fall closed,
it is not a restful sleep.
    I dream of distances
        greater than I can measure,
    a world made of water
and almost nothing else,
    when you really think about it.

Sea Air

By the time morning arrives,
the *sea air* makes me new again,
staining my skin
and tangling in my hair.

The last sign of land
has long since disappeared
so that *the ocean is only an ocean,*
with nothing and no one for miles.

I watch the first light
as it *dances*
across the choppy waves,
and I do not notice my tears
until the wind makes them cool,
icy against my cheek.
I watch the world seem to unravel
in shades of blue and spun gold.

And I think, that maybe,
though things are so difficult,
it is always worth trying again.

Percentages

More than 70 percent
of the surface of the earth
is only the far-reaching oceans.
That accounts for around 97 percent
of all the water on Earth.[14]

All the while, in a world of such scale,
I am only ever one person
who herself is 70 percent water.

It's difficult to believe that anything I do
could have much importance
in the grand scheme of things.

But imagine being a human
who could swim without fins
and fly with no wings.

When I consider the way my kind
have built a way to achieve
all the impossibilities,
I think, really: nothing is impossible at all.

Not even that humans
could soon enough conquer
70 percent of the ocean
and 70 perfect of everything.

Where We're Going

"Where we're going
is where the going gets tough,"
a woman from the crew,
who introduces herself as Sarah,
tells me as we sail far out to sea.

"We're right on track," she says,
"to find what keeps
a sailor up at night,
if he loves the ocean
as much as he claims to."

"And you ought to," says Jones,
who has sailed for all of his life.

I admit, I'm just slightly *afraid.*

I've started believing
that anything is possible,
and not always for the better.
The further we travel
from when I last saw land,
the darker and deeper
the rolling waves become.
The clearer the truth is
that humans have only
just grazed the water's surface,
exploring and charting
a mere five percent of the blue.[15]

I do not get lost in the quiet and calm.
I trust the oceans for all of their power
and know it is greater than my own.

I stand to watch

the seas rolling by,
and never do I doubt
that my fate always rests
in the shapes of the waves
that crash when they fall.

Acid and Heat

A terrifying 90 percent
of global warming happens
out here in the oceans,[16]
the waters heating up
until ice starts to thaw
and the water level
rises higher than it was.

All at once, the high CO_2
of the last 200 years
since the industrial revolution
sends carbon pooling
into the water like a sink.

I look down on the waters as they turn to acid.

Until the marine creatures
with their exoskeletons
fail to adapt fast enough
and cannot survive
the changing seas
in time to avoid
E X T I N C T I O N.

Rising Sea Levels

It's so subtle
it's almost imperceptible,
the way the sea levels climb
a little higher every year.
As far back as the 1980s,
India's Lohachara Island
sunk below the surface,
declared disappeared
by December in 2006.[17]

Others will follow.

The low-lying nations
and the people who live there,
with their homes and families,
cultures and livelihoods.
All of it can be washed away
in the instant too many
it takes for us to act.

Rising sea levels
climb higher and higher,
and one day, I fear,
they might wash
us all away.

Another lost city,
like the story of Atlantis,
forever buried beneath the waves.

The Island

Soon, I think I see land
in the distance,
slowly moving closer.
I squint my eyes,
but I cannot find
the shape of an island
without jagged edges.

Time brings truth into sharp focus.

I watch the mass of could-have-been land
edging closer every minute.

The nearer we draw,
the more pieces I find,
floating and twisting
along the water's surface
and surely deep below.

A million tiny pieces of plastic
and at least a million more.

Enough junk and waste and great mistakes
that I cannot find anything else.

Enough garbage waste clouding the waters
that it had me believing this place was a country.

We truly are done for, I think to myself. *Aren't we?*

Great Pacific Garbage Patch

"Welcome," Sarah tells me,
"to the Great Pacific Garbage Patch."

Here, the water spins a vortex
that draws waste closer
as if it is a magnet
for everything gone wrong.

Here, over 80,000 tonnes
of plastic floats above the waves,
enough to build 500 jumbo jets,
waiting ready to take flight.[18]

The Great Pacific Garbage Patch
is far from a holiday island,
far from the kind of place
you go to sunbake on vacation.

Here, there is plenty waste enough
to account for 250 pieces of debris
for every human who walks the earth.

Around me, it swirls and stagnates.
I look around, and I cannot decide
whether I'm angry or just overwhelmed.

Once, these seas were clear and free,
a place for the animals swimming and living.
Now it's difficult to imagine anything could live here at all.

Life in Plastic

Life in plastic stretches further
than my tired eyes can see.
For three times the size of France,
caught in the clockwise spiral
of four spinning currents colliding.[19]

What's worse than what I can see
is everything that I can't.
Millions and trillions of tiny pieces,
too microscopic to be found.
These are the invisible weapons
that creep their way through waters
and burrow into the food supply.

"Some scientists believe," says Sarah,
"the average person eats five grams
of miserable microplastics each week."[20]

A shudder dances across my shoulders.
Still and quiet, I stare out to sea.
"Isn't there anything we can do?"
I whisper, voice hoarse from salty air.

"That's what we're hoping,"
says a member of the crew.
"That someone like you
might just care enough
to try and make a difference."

All That Sinks

"And that's not accounting
for all that sinks," says Sarah
of the murky, muddy waters
in this sorry ocean gyre.

Forget the waste way up above
when oceanographers believe
as much as 70 percent of debris
sinks low to the deep ocean floor.[21]

Little by little, this island of waste
begins sinking below the surface.
To the places where the sun gives out
and water pressure climbs high,
where the dark and dense waters
are home to so many marine creatures,
at least until the stomachs fill up
with all too much plastic,
until the mounds of debris
steal away all the oxygen.

At least until it's too late
for anything to survive here anymore.

Depth and Scope

"Every piece of plastic
that ever was made
exists somewhere still,"
Sarah tells me.
"Unless it burns with fumes
that cloud the atmosphere."

For at least 500 years,
this waste stays strong
and refuses to biodegrade.[22]
To think halfway to 1,000
is long enough for history
but not for a world healing.

Every day, mega factories
churn out more waste
that rely on fossil fuels
and toxic chemicals
good for nothing but harm.

Every day, this whole world
gets a little bit fuller.
Another tiny piece of a problem
starts a slow journey to someplace like here.

        The spinning island
        of growing waste
                that floats and sinks
                in the middle of the ocean.

Biodegrade

When the plastic
won't break down,
it's difficult to find
a decent solution.

Where will it go if not to the ocean?
Where will it gather if not out here?
Or else in mounds of landfill, crowding,
stacked up high and buried low?

I begin to wonder
who has the power
to face up to a problem
like this, if anyone.
Then I realise
I shouldn't be asking
where we will send
the plastic to keep it
away from the water ways.

Instead, I should wonder
why we keep making more
when clearly,
there is plenty
already.

Deteriorating

Even as I stand
here to watch,
I swear I notice
the ocean crash, crumble,
just a little at a time.

I harness all my fire and energy
as if I am set for a fight.

But as the ocean deteriorates fast,
I can't help feeling helpless,
unsure of what to do next.

"How can we do anything at all?"
I hear myself asking whoever will hear it.
"When there's nothing but devastation
and not a single solution in sight?"

The crew clap each other on the backs
and promise every great feat
begins with a little at a time.
Still, I feel blinded by pointlessness.
with nothing but hope
that slowly is fading out.

Oil Spill

Just as I think
there might still
be a chance,
I catch sight
of another boat
not far in the distance.

Poorly managed.
Barely maintained.
These are the vessels
that put the poor oceans
to a sentence of misery.

Oily streaks stain
the surface of the sea
in black, inky swirls
that shimmer in the light
in all the colours
of a rainbow.

Just another oil spill,
like *just* another piece of plastic
and *just* another day
where we all sit back and do nothing.

All this is to say
that *just* isn't enough
because someday soon,
it will *just* be too late.

Rage

And so I let oil
and the plastic it builds
spill and gather
all around me.
All the while, I wait,
biting my tongue
as rage rises high
and drowns out the air
in my aching lungs.

Always, people say
that you shouldn't be angry,
but I cannot cave now
to the hollow sadness
when there is work to be done.

My anger and my spite
drive me forward
as I stay true to my resolve
that a long list of lifetimes
worth of human survival
cannot be about to end
just like this.

With all of the fury
that I have in my heart,
I rage against the ending.

Life on Land

I am forced to think bigger
than the waves in the sea
and wonder the future
of life on land.
I look far beyond
the deep blue
for signs of food systems
failing when the fish all wash up.

I look for evidence of plastic on my plate.
Of the Great Lakes that serve
40 million people enough to drink.[23]

I think of the coasts
that clutter with debris
and can no longer be a place
to clear my messy mind.
And of the nutrients
meant to cycle through the water.

The ocean plants
consuming enough CO_2
so we don't all burst into flames
until it captures so much carbon
that the water turns acid,
and the seashells fizzle,
E F F E R V E S C I N G
until there is nothing left.

Mission

"It seems a little hopeless, January,"
my fellow passengers tell me
with a wobble in their voices
before the words all give out.
"But I think, just maybe,
there's still a little hope
left for us yet."

I hold my mission true,
like a life raft set to capture me
before I sink below.

I think to myself that I barely know anything at all.
But what I know now is the most important thing of all.

What I know is that today
is no time yet for quitting.
That the battle ahead
is fierce and unyielding
and bound to be brutal,
and in these critical moments,
it has only just begun.

I suppose, in the grand scheme of things,
the city's way here doesn't matter so much
as the way the city must find its way out.

Salt

My journal of poems remembers
all the places I have been.
Here, the salt air stains pages
with the lingering realness
of a life spent at sea.

But that is not all.

Because tiny pieces
of plastic waste
sometimes find
their way onboard.
And I am reminded
how far there remains
to travel towards
something better.

When I find these fragments
of dirt and debris,
I do not let them
escape back to the sea.
Instead, I plaster them
to poetry pages,
where over again,
they tell me,
what matters out here
and *why.*

Horizon

I catch my breath
as I watch the horizon
escape from the night
to the golden tones
of dawn breaking.
I swear I hear it *shatter*.

I watch the world
as it seems to unravel
and imagine I can feel
the earth turning
until I grow dizzy
when it sways
beneath my tired feet.

I watch the horizon
with an ache in my chest
that feels like a *poem*
I can't string into words.

All day long, I watch
the edge of the horizon.
Slowly, we move towards it.
And as we chase the climbing sun,
I *wish* for the *light* in the *darkness*.

Whale Song

I stay until nightfall,
when the world is dark
and eerily quiet.
By the faint glow
of glittering starlight,
I carve truth into tales
and fill pages
with poems
and *hope*.

When I pause
for a moment,
when my pen
stops to still,
there is nothing out here
except for the rush
of the waves
and somewhere more distant,
a melodic symphony
of voices unmistakeably
whale song.

Poetry Pages

When there is nothing else left,
I turn back to my poems.
My hands are too cold
to keep the pen in my grip,
and yet I force the ink to paper
in shaking, just legible script.

Pages fill with stories
more than just my own.

As I write, I remember
all the people I've met,
all that I've learned so far.

Soon, I will run out of pages.
Words will give way to quiet.

But for now, I keep writing.
Unsure of who will read.
But certain that there is a purpose.
That poems have power worth believing.
That time has not just yet run out.

Blue

Jones says the ocean
matters more than we know
because of the things
that we don't yet.
"On the good days," he says,
"it brings food to the shore
and money to island communities.
In the bad times," says Jones,
"the ocean is violent
and brings pollution
that moves past the coast."

From waterborne illness
to toxic algal blooms,
I learn that the water
is rarely at fault.
And yet it is powerful,
much more than we know.

For saving us
or breaking us down.

Which? It's the question
that stays on my tongue.

Will the seas rescue our planet or drag it under?

Calling to the Wind

One more time, I call
my voice to the wind
until it echoes enough
to think I hear answers.
It spirals around me
as if a *hurricane*
of my own making.

I hold my small book
with its pages of poems
in the fist that I make
of my right hand.
I shout myself out
and then shout some more.
Soon, the whole world
can hear me,
for as far as it goes.
I call to the wind
loud enough
that it answers.

It reminds me
that all is not lost.

Northbound

I don't know if we travel
for days, weeks, or months.
But a little at a time,
we edge to the north.

So slowly as to be
almost imperceptible,
the temperature falls
to an icy chill
that tints my skin
a rosy red
and numbs my fingers
with the cold.

So slowly and carefully
that I barely notice,
I feel the waters
give way to frozen stillness,
find the movements
of my body dull
and drawn out.

I while away the hours
staring out to sea,
squinting my eyes
as I look for land.
Then, in the distance,
I catch sight of islands
that aren't made of plastic.

With every passing moment,
the outlines become a little clearer
until they overtake the empty horizon,
replacing water with solid ground.

I track lines of maps

and a magnetic compass
until we sail north
almost as far
as the world
will take us.

A Song for the Sea

I find the coastline
in ghostly shades
of silver-blue ice
as the old boat slows
to a final stop.

The ocean breeze soon buries me.
The roaring wind cuts out sight and sound.
At last, we've crossed the ocean.

We dock at a half-frozen port,
where I stumble on my legs
made for the uneven waves.

I turn around once more
to find the seas before I leave them.
I wait time enough to know what I'll miss
before I step away, and the old boat leaves without me.

I raise my right hand in a captain's salute
and watch good friends salute to me too.

Then I turn on my heel,
and the ocean is gone,
and because I know better,
I never look back.
Only whisper the opening notes
of a song for the sea.

ARCTIC

Welcome to the Arctic

The boat turns and sails away,
but I do not turn to watch it go.
I stand alone in the cold and the ice.
In the shivery weather,
under cover of half darkness,
I watch a new landscape unfold.

Tiny houses not far from the pier.
Ice floating on the shallowest water.

It seems I have reached
the very edge of the world,
where I feel just a stumble
might send me falling

      up...

           up...

                up...

and into the midst of the stars.

I make myself taller,
make my muscles feel strong.
"Welcome to the Arctic,"
I whisper to myself
as I hope it treats me well.

Cabin Fever

First, I am walking
across the frozen ground
until I am too cold
to remember
my own name.

Moments later,
without remembering
how I got there,
I am sheltered
in the warmth of a cabin
with plush armchairs
and a fire in the hearth.
There is a thick blanket
draped over my shoulders
by the couple who live here
and say their names
are Erik and Astrid.

I hold a mug of hot chocolate
until my hands thaw out.
And I think I already know
how this place could be a home.

Clear Skies

I don't think I've known
skies quite so clear.

Time hovers somewhere
between winter and summer
so that the all-day night
will soon give way
to the midnight sun.

Strung up by starlight
and wispy grey clouds
is a ribbon of purple,
green, and aquamarine.

The spectrum of lights
that burst into colour
when energised particles
from the burning hot sun
reach Earth's upper atmosphere
and collide at great speeds
of 45 million miles an hour
so that the magnetic field
is forced to redirect
the dizzying light to the poles.[24]

"Wow." I breathe out.
I am so far from home.
And I've never found anything
quite so *beautiful*.

A Place Like Home

On Svalbard, the island
I call a temporary home,
there are just over
2,000 living local.[25]

Off the coast of Norway
and halfway to the North Pole,
this place calls to settlers
from all around the globe.
I find myself staying
in the heart of Longyearbyen,
the northernmost settlement
in the whole world.
So close to what seems
like the end of the world,
there are food shops
and libraries
and museums.
Astrid informs me
I have not long missed
the Arctic Film Festival
that takes place
in the Kulturhuset each year.[26]

The people are welcoming
at the high edge of everything.
And it isn't true, yet I feel I belong.

Sparing

We are sparing, here,
with use of supplies,
in the fight to protect
our home base.

"The mainland is close,"
says Erik confidently.
"Enough to bring in
anything we need.
But out here, in the wild,
why take more
than what matters?
When the world
barely has enough to give?"

We are careful and strategic
and never too greedy.
And soon,
I am thinking
how this all
could be better
if more people
had these same ideas
a little further afield.

The Biome

The tundra, I learn,
is a unique biome,
where it's easy to think
the cold must mean rain.
And yet, this place
gets only about
as much rainfall
as a desert.
At least that
used to be the truth.[27]

All year round,
the ground below the top soil
is supposed to be frozen,
when times are good.
As far as I search,
there are barely any signs of life,
a distinct lack of biodiversity
because so little is strong enough
to survive in the wilderness,
in cold quite so brutal as this is.

Snow

I never was fond
of the ice and snow,
but soon enough,
I grow to love it
as my footprints bury deep.

Here, the flat ground
is a great expanse
of frozen white,
like a Christmas card
with none of the trimmings.

I talk to the locals.
I learn my way around.
And slowly, I discover the island.

Every day,
I run, and I leap.
I am bolder
and a little bit braver
and more certain
that this place
is worth saving.

Ice Melt

But ice is melting
at an alarming rate,
and though it is cold,
it is warmer than it should be.

"Every year, the air loses a little of its chill," says Erik.
"And more of the ice melts, adds to the height of the sea."

In a year alone, says Astrid,
the summer months melt
over 100 billion metric tons
of icy water, pouring
into the ocean,
where it is no wonder
sea levels are climbing.[28]

"What if it melts?" I ask.
"What will happen then?"

Erik and Astrid tell me
what once were anomalies
are now a common affair.
"The Arctic is warming
twice as fast as the global average
or maybe double again."[29]

"If it melts, then it melts," they say solemnly.
"And the whole of the world might just melt too."

Weather Station

Svalbard is home to a research station
that is further north than any other.
Here, the scientists gather often
to share their data and analyse change.
Here, the climate is changing faster
than anyone knows what to do with.
In fact, on Svalbard, the data reveals
the weather is warming many times
faster than the rest of the world.
Last summer was the hottest on record.
This year, we expect another leap.
But the heat is not all of the trouble.
The data shows patterns in jagged graphs
that map out a rise in rough storms.
Once, the rain failed here, hardly falling,
and now we hear thunder roll in
from the clouds we can't quite trust.[30]
As I help crunch the numbers,
I always am thinking
of the tipping point
I am sure
we must reach
sometime soon
and how
we might fall
over the edge.

Habitats > Adaptation

Sleek and powerful,
the polar bears roam,
a little less freely than they did.
As it turns out, habitats change
faster than adaptation can keep up with.

Who could evolve
as fast as the climate
that changes again,
year after year?

Too quickly, the ice
slips away and vanishes
until there is nowhere left
for sea ice seal hunting
or raising polar bear cubs.
So they struggle and hunger
and grow thinner each day.
Scientists predict
as much as two thirds
of all the world's polar bears
could be gone by 2050.[31]
And after that, there's no telling
how long the thinning ice
will give to the bears
before the whole species goes extinct.

The Collapse

And if ice collapses into the sea
as one sweeping fall, it's all *over*.

At least for the people
in low-lying towns
when the water climbs
and pushes under.

As all the ice thaws,
there's less space for bright.
Land shrinks and gives way
to near blackness of deep waters.
And dark colours keep
more heat than the light.
So the warmth of the sun
will be drawn here
and trapped by a blanket
made of methane,
carbon dioxide,
and nitrous oxide.

And sure enough,
temperatures will soar.
Enough to melt
some more of the ice
and make the world
warmer still.

Buried by Permafrost

And all of this is not to mention
the thawing permafrost
that does so much more
than just change the terrain.

As what's frozen thaws out, so does what's preserved.

Still more carbon will be
released from ice
and into the atmosphere,
alongside old viruses,
like the Bubonic Plague.
Alongside old microbes
and chemicals leaching
into the space all around
that is already struggling
and barely can take
yet another hit.

Which should we fear most?
I find myself wondering.

Pandemic? Extinction? Hunger?

Or a world
that starts burning
like one great fire
that is bigger
than us all?

The Arctic Tree Line

Then there is the tree line,
the northernmost place
where towering trees
know how to grow.
A little more northern
with each passing year.
Chasing after me,
as I chase someplace away.

Astrid says she remembers
trees at a distance, now racing forward,
because the soils are warm.
Rumour has it, the tree line
leaps northwards again
by 40 or 50 metres a year.[32]

Soon, the white polar landscape
will give way to the green
in a place never built to be a forest.

Just like in the Amazon,
where I watched the rush
of rainforest turning
to a savannah...

The biomes are changing
and switching their places,
and I fear some, like the tundra,
soon will fade out altogether.

The First Strike

This is the first strike
of a fast-changing climate,
driven by ice melting
to dark waters
that drink up
solar energies
until the earth heats
a notch higher.

Here in the Arctic,
a great frozen ocean,
the ice is returning
now to the sea.
I look all around,
and I can't help but view
what happens here
as a sign of what's next.

This isn't an island
but the top of the world
before the disaster
trickles,
slowly...

A L L
      THE
WAY
      DOWN.

Before My Eyes

Before my eyes,
the tundra changes
its shape again.
As the summer months
begin to approach,
the slow rising sun
starts to remodel
the landscape,
cutting out ice
and replacing it
with meltwater.

"Sometimes, it seems just a day is enough,"
Astrid tells me when I ask whether she notices
how everything is always changing.
"For now, this is home," Erik says lowly.
But I hear in the silence the words he won't say.

That I'm not the only one planning for fleeing.
Home, but he isn't sure how much longer it can be.

What Next?

Then Astrid turns to me,
as if I have the answers.
"What happens next?" she asks, her voice high.
Her fingers fix onto my wrist like a vice.

She and Erik always planned
to live here all their lives,
but Astrid says this home is changing so fast,
she barely recognises it.
And by the time they reach old age
and plan to settle down,
she isn't sure what this home might look like.

"What should we do so the Arctic's not over?
How can we not lose this place? Our home?"

I wish I had answers
that weren't empty promises.
Instead, I can only smile gently.
"There's nothing to do but keep trying for longer,"
I whisper, though the words ring like something hollow.

"I can't promise to fix it. I'll promise to try.
To make the suits and machines take some notice."

Before...
        ...our time...
                ...is up.

Fossil Fuels

And then I watch the shadows
not far off in the distance.
"The government won't stop it,"
says Astrid, mouth pressed in a line.
"In fact, they're giving permits.
and every day, there's more drilling
for gas and oil buried beyond
the boundaries of old treaties."

Fossil fuel energy companies
go digging for power
beneath the fragile ice.
I watch them fight and pillage.

"There's plenty of scope
for it all to go wrong," says Erik.
"And if not, then we all wait
for the damage of the decades,
when the wildlife dies out
and what's left of the ice crumbles."

After that, I know the sorry truth.
That someday, there won't be
an Arctic to worry about.
That someday, all of this
will just be more sea,
stretching as far north as anything
before it turns south again.

Senselessly

Erik goes on to tell me
that some of the diggers
are as bold as to freeze
the permafrost over,
not to help but to hinder,
to find just long enough
so that machines
can keep drilling for cash.

That's right.

The great leaders
of energy supply
and carbon emissions
are prepared to help
only when it's personal
and gain is at stake.

And never mind all
the next generations
who won't care for power
and electrified houses
so much as they care
for their sad, fragile lives.

Senseless, it seems.
As if nothing else matters
but making a dime.

All I Promise

"Just don't give up on us,"
says Astrid when I ask
what she thinks I should do.
So I promise I won't.

Then I set about trying to figure out how
I am going to keep all of these promises,
the ones that I scatter like a trail of breadcrumbs,
all the way around this whole world.

All I promise is not quite enough.
That I won't give up or give out
until it's over for good.
Only if no one gives up on me,
on not just the Arctic
but all the places beyond it.

I tell Astrid and Erik
about the forest, the desert, the sea.

That they are not alone.
This is bigger than all of us.
And someone must stand up and shout out.

Though I try to pretend I am not frightened,
increasingly, I worry that this *someone* might have to be *me*.

Migration Season

Soon, it is migration season,
when the roaming polar bears
quit wandering the island
of the archipelago
and follow the sea ice
as it reaches north-east.

Migrating, the same way that I do.

I watch their outlines in the distance
and think they look a little too thin.

"Never approach a polar bear," says Astrid.
"They are too smart and too hungry and too dangerous too."

Never mind: I am happy to stand back and see
the way that they move across the land.

But there is less sea ice
than last year or the year before that.
And I watch the bears struggle
to leap and to hunt.

Survival
is perched
on *thin* ice.

Sketches

As I step forward,
poems turn to sketches
when I can't find the words.
The pages fill fast
with linework,
the shape of an iceberg
and the shadow of the sun.

Here, in this place, where time has no meaning,
I often stay writing late into the night
and until morning rocks back around again.

I never know truth
before I look it in the eyes,
but I trust in a lyric
pieced together with care
to tell the world
what it needs to know.

The Beginnings of a Plan

I set to work
on the beginnings
of a plan
with rough edges
and not
enough centre.

In the blurry way
of sight without lenses,
I watch dull-edged shapes fall together.

Soon, I know not
just what I should do
or how to approach it from here.

But I know I am sure
of a purpose for planning.
That the beginnings of a plan
start with my poetry journal
and the words the world
should be ready to hear.

A Little Brighter

Just barely, the weather
becomes a bit warmer,
grazing towards 7°C.

Slowly, I venture
a little way further
and begin to explore
the sweeping land.

Ever so slightly,
the dark fades from the sky.
I find a few less of the stars.

As the island finds light,
native wildlife roams too.
I feel my spirits rise higher
until I wonder how the people
who live here ever make it so long
in the crush of winter dark.

Resistance

I look up to the sky
and watch the stars
blink out of sight
as slowly, deep black
fades away to fresh lilac,
soon turning a crisp and clear blue.

Clouds tinge in tones of pink and gold
just as dazzling as the Northern Lights
now the sun starts shining through.
I let light guide my way.

Astrid and Erik
gather their friends,
and we soon form a makeshift
R E S I S T A N C E.

No one is certain
what steps to take next,
except more of the same is no option.

Even as land made of thin ice
begins to crash down around us,
we do not lose the ground we've gained
or the power that makes us stand tall and rebel.

A fight is unfurling,
and no one is backing down this time.

The Sun That Never Sets

Summer approaches
at a sprint, not a stroll.

And soon, the days
brighten sharply
until the sun
finds its place
to the highest point
in a clear blue sky,
and it does not
try setting again.

In the dazzling light
of the midnight sun
that glistens
all hours of the night,
my coat is warm enough
and the heat
turns ice to water.
I have no more doubts.
I know what I must do.
I prepare for my
goodbyes.

I follow along to the ends of the world,
prepare to leap into icy waters and the great unknown.

Bidding Goodbyes

I leave the archipelago
and let it fade away
with just a final wave
and a few tearful goodbyes.
I make all my promises
and swear to lead the fight.
Before I know it,
I'm watching the ice
speed away from sight.

Before I know it,
the tree line is gone
and the drills
and the weather station
along with it.

Before I know it,
my eyes are fixed
solely on what lies ahead.
I do not miss
the frozen tundra
so much as I wish
I could help it.

So that is what I'm going to do.

Talisman

As I race towards the airport,
I hold my journal like a talisman
until it leaves prints across my skin.
I feel the weight of my poems
rest in the palm of my hand.
I feel the weight of the world
fall upon my shoulders.

I do not turn to look behind me.
I do not wish to give up or give in.
I trace my fingers along poetry pages
and believe in the words I have found so far.
I believe in the words I'm still chasing.
I believe in their power, if I wield my words well,
to do something in this world that so needs it.

I do not wonder what happened.
I focus on what happens next.

A Song for the Arctic

My heart is aching in my chest
as I let the Arctic fade away
and become the land behind me.
I turn around to watch it go,
to see the island grow smaller
and finally disappear from sight.
I hold my journal in one hand
and my pen in the other,
and with every mile
that drags me away,
I stain my skin with ink.
Just under my breath,
I whisper my truth
so that I can hear it
and believe it is true.
"I promise to help,"
I tell whoever listens.
"And I swear that I'll write
a song for the Arctic."

SAVANNAH

The Grasslands

A new landscape appears,
so different I barely recognise it,
a far cry from the barren cold of the Arctic ice.

I watch the earth change shape all around me.
I do not ask it to be familiar.

The savannah is rolling grasslands,
      stretching further than I can see.
            The shadows of trees and shrubs
      only popping up now and then
          so that each that stands alone
      casts a far-reaching shadow
across the dusty soil.

The air smells of mud
and marsh grasses
and maybe magnolias
as just a trace.

I think this place is a question.
And I seek to find the answers.

The savannah is rolling grasslands,
and for now, it welcomes me home.

Welcome

The locals welcome me
with open arms
and extra plates
and stories about their home.

I look all around me
and admire the richness
of this vast, sweeping land.

The sun is warm on my skin
that has almost forgotten how not to freeze.

The coarse grasses brush by
and rustle lightly in the wind.

I always think I hear footsteps
of animals wandering far.
I tilt my head up to the sky
and close my eyes and realise.

I am someway halfway
between forest and desert
and a million miles
from anyplace,
anywhere else.

N O W H E R E
is a place
like this one.

New Strength

I set out to explore,
following the horizon.
I quickly find
a new strength,
as if clawed up
from the fabric
of my spirit.

Here, I am brave and bold and sure.

"What brings you here?" asks Amahle,
a man around my age with autumn eyes.
"And what will make you stay?" asks Zuri,
his teen sister, wise beyond her years.

"I am here to learn,"
I tell them with confidence.
"Enough to try
and understand the earth,
enough that all of us
can band together now
and help the savannah
and the planet it shares."

Built for Survival

The landscape out here
is built for survival,
made to tolerate
warm temperatures
and moderate rainfall.
Made to make it
through fire
and drought.

Evidence appears at most every turn.

No empty spaces
where nothing will live.
Here, there are footsteps
carved into the dirt
from wandering wildlife
I don't think I would recognise.

The dry, sweeping lands
are a map of diversity,
built for survival
and for all of us
still *surviving*.

Phoenix

The savannah is a phoenix
rising from the flames,
the product of fires
that maintain biodiversity.

A savannah blaze
keeps tree cover low
and stops surrounding forests
from growing into more grasslands.

Scientists say that fires here help
to cycle nutrients and halt species invading.
The flames keep the savannah
still fit for fighting,
clearing out old matter
and making way
for a landscape,
rich and varied,
that revives itself
all over again.

Flora and Fauna

A herd of elephants pauses to cool off at a watering hole.
A maned lion rests in the shade from the afternoon sun.

The savannah is mostly star and lemon grasses
dotted with baobab and jackalberry trees.

Even so, the savannah
suffers a little each day.
Around half of vegetation
has turned to farms and ranches,
for agricultural products
that will not stay here long
before they're shipped
to the European industries.[33]

Even in the spaces
where the grass has not thinned
where trees are not felled,
there are too many plants
introduced from abroad
and not enough locals
to keep the ecosystem thriving
and the native animals still eating well.

Habitat loss appears at each turn,
and it's difficult to think
how the savannah itself
is ever supposed to keep up.

Only Four Percent

Around the globe, less than four percent
of original tallgrass prairie survives still.[34]

Scattered remains by the roadside
or bunched together in an effort for restoration.
The healthiest, best-watered ecosystem
is one of the world's most endangered
as ploughing and clearing take hold.

The savannah is poached and parched.
Animals hunted for resources and wares
until they begin a march to extinction.
Land that dries out more than it should,
too harsh even for the sturdiest grasses.
I watch the way that ecological threats
engulf the landscape all around me
and think it all could be avoidable
if only the way we humans live
could take enough time out
to know what's worth saving,
as a priority above the next big thing.

Now I can see that action is critical,
that too late is too soon to arrive.

Future of the Forest

I am struck by a subtle sadness
as my memory wanders
to imagine this place
as the future of the forest.

I recall the forest elders
and their fears of a shift
that would sweep down the trees
and turn them to grasslands.

It is difficult to imagine
and yet not difficult at all.

The truth is, when I think of it,
when I know the impact
of the most harmful industries,
I do not think it unlikely
that the rainforest could turn
into a place just like this,
beautiful too
and just as rich
and valuable
but never
what the Amazon
should be.

The People and Their Stories

The people and their stories
tell me they're counting on change
as I trek closer towards shining sunbeams.

Sometimes, words are quiet,
but I always guess their meaning.

In the earliest hours of morning
and until the sun sets at night,
the savannah surrounds me
like a circle of spirits,
and soon, I know it well.

I cannot miss the subtle signs
that all is not as well as it seems.
When booming voices turn
to whispers in the night.
When dinner comes in pieces,
and there aren't enough to share.

"We need help here, January," says Zuri,
when she thinks I have fallen asleep.

I know they do. Just like the others.
Even though I don't know what I can do
to make the difference they so badly need.

Unsustainable

"Don't convert the African savannah
into only agricultural lands."
I want to shout this message
from the tops of the trees
until someone can hear it.
Because each day, I wander,
and I see the farms finding
new places in degrading soils.

I watch the land tilling, too many times over
for the earth to stay healthy
enough for anything good
to keep on growing.
Another few seasons,
and unsustainable practices
could push parts of the soil
far over the edge.

The Signs

I see the signs all around me,
clear as the crystalline daylight.
So it's hard to understand
how the rest of the world won't see them too.

The savannah is a hardy place.
Strong enough to withstand.

But this truth is, if no one pays mind,
soon, this place will struggle
against damages that could last a few lifetimes.

Why is no one sustaining what we need to survive?

Soil Health

As the soil health deteriorates,
so do the food systems.
Monocropping
and over-tilling
force the earth
to degrade
so that it's not fit
for growing anymore.
Pesticides poison
the earth and the air
and the wildlife
that wanders
these lands.

In an effort to keep
earning for now,
too many folk
are too willing
to sacrifice safety
and the world
the day after
tomorrow.

Someday a Desert

In the heat of the sunlight I follow,
the savannah becomes hotter and drier
until I swear I see it slowly changing shape.

What is next for speeding transitions
that turn the land into something new?

I can't help thinking that someday,
the savannah might be a desert,
the same way the tundra could be a forest
and the forest could be a savannah.

In my lifetime,
the earth is changing
in just the blink of an eye,
fast enough that I might miss it
if I dare to look away.

How to Help

I find power
that must before
have buried
deep beneath
my sun-stung skin.
When I know how to help,
I am brighter and braver.
With my hands in the soil,
I am not so hopeless.

The days are long and arduous,
dragging on until
I think I must have missed
at least a few turns of the sun.
But while I am working
out here in the heat,
I finally feel like
I'm not just the problem
but part of a solution.

Like nothing is so insurmountable
that it cannot be fixed by time and care
and a willingness for people to change.
Before the climate does.

Stand United

"We must stand united,"
Amahle tells me, earnest.
"Not against each other
or the rest of the world."

And I think of the people
who may not know better,
their world-breaking deals
and their rotten bank notes.

"United," says Zuri.
"Not at odds or against.
Don't lose yourself
in the act fighting
and forget its purpose."

I harness my fury,
and I keep it on leash.
So that I can stop fighting
against the powers that be
and convince them that truly,
I'm not fighting against anything.
Instead, I'm just fighting for us all.

When the World is Wilder

If we do enough work
over enough years
and enough space,
Zuri says there's hope
for the land to recover,
For the populations
of wild animals to boom
when there is plenty
more grass left for grazing.

"It's not much," says Amahle,
with bright, starry eyes.
"But it's something better
than nothing at all."

When the world is wilder,
it finds its own feet and stands strong.
We can trust in the planet
to treat herself with care.

Out here in the grasslands,
I give up, out on questions.

In the dirt, fields, and flowers,
I work tirelessly in faith
that just like Amahle says,
doing something is better
than quitting now.

Even When

Even when it seems useless,
I often work late into the night,
for some way to be helpful
and for something to do
that isn't just sitting and waiting.

When I am not labouring
to rewild the wetlands
or rotate the crops
before they give out,
I am writing.

Even when the odds seem
so close to impossible
that it's pointless,
Zuri and Amahle
always have their faith,
and they remind me
to believe in hope persevering.

Here to There

From here to there,
I understand impact,
the far-reaching
implications
of the savannah.

The grasslands
that are shrinking
are home to a quarter
of the whole population
the world over,
and that's not to mention
the thousands of plants
and animals roaming these plains.[35]

I watch silhouettes
of vast-numbered species
parading their shadows
by the orange light of sunset.

And from here to there,
I understand how
this place matters
maybe more
to the world beyond it
than to the savannah itself.

By the Light of the Moon

"What would you do
if anything was possible?"
Amahle stays awake
long after dark
to watch the stars with me.

I hum.

"I'm not sure," I tell him honestly.
"Maybe just the simple things,
like mapping out constellations
until I fell asleep."

Amahle knows the stories
of the shapes in the night sky.
By the light of the moon,
he reaches up and traces patterns
in the gaps in the moonbeams.

He tells me grand tales
about ancient deities
who lived and loved
and carved out a difference.

Eventually, his soft voice lulls me to sleep.
And I dream I am the sky.

Spark

On two feet and truth,
I tour the land,
enough to see
what it represents.

I think careful and clever
as often as I can
as I search for a way
to spark change.

Just one tiny spark
is plenty for fire.

And I'm ready
to burn up
a *blaze*.

I Become Her

Daylight is rich and golden,
and I never take it for granted.
Because even when the savannah nights
feel long and dark and lonely,
I am comforted in the quiet
by the sound I almost hear
of the earth spinning on its axis
and guiding another sunrise home.

And when there is little more
to all that I am
but the dirt on my cheeks
and my ink-stained hands.
I hold my head up high
and face the sun or the starbeams.

Resilience: I become her.

Earthquake

It's an intangible thing, tricky to name.
But I know it deep in my bones.

Change speeds like a freight train,
and my hand is on the throttle.

A shift is on its way. I swear it.
I steady my balance, feet flat to the ground.

As if I am waiting for an earthquake.

End of Chapter

I can't wait here forever,
and what's new races closer.

The sun seems to call to me, and I listen.

"We'll miss you around here," says Zuri.
"But I think it's true you have to go.
You have to have something to say
that might make at least a small difference,
while there's still some time left on the clock."

I approach my last few journal pages.
I read over my words, and I think a chapter is ending.

What's next? I soon wonder.
Then I know the answer.

The rest of the story begins.

Sunburn

Once more, I feel the sunlight
sting my sunburned skin.
I raise my hand in a half salute
to wave the people goodbye.

I march on light footsteps
over the flat ground
until the animals disappear,
and I can't hear the sound
of a song from a campsite
or a lion roaring.

I let the heat empower me
to trust in my truth
and an honest purpose,
to make my way back
to the city I abandoned
and to make it
someplace different
from what it was
last time I knew it well.

Duty

Then I am the setting sun,
sinking beneath the horizon.
I leave the savannah
with a sense of duty,
a responsibility
that I am its voice.

So even though,
I might cough
and might stutter,
I refuse to give in
to the call of silence.

Not when so many people and places
rely on me now to speak loud
until someone listens. I will shout out
until the words are all gone.

Because I owe it to the places that matter.

A Song for the Savannah

I watch the grasslands
sprawl for miles
and out of sight.
I let them fall behind
until they disappear,
and I can no longer see
the shape of a sunset
crowded out
by the shadows
of old trees
and roaming wildlife.

As I begin
my journey home
back to the city,
I think I hear
music on the air.
I promise with all
the conviction I have
that I will write
a song for the savannah.

The Darkest Days

The city unfolds before me,
but I can no longer find it
a space for belonging.
Old friends welcome me home.
My sister tries but doesn't understand.

Some of these are my darkest days.
I am alone to feel useless and afraid.
Hopelessness sometimes seems
as though it consumes me,
a cloud in the air that calls me its thunder.

On the darkest days,
it is difficult to look for any light.
So I picture the sun shared by the skies
in all of the places I've been.

And soon, I remember,
as dark as days seem,
I am never as alone as I believe.

Friends

I remind myself of my friends,
in the middle of the ocean
and in lands far away,
buried by the forest,
warmed by savannah sunlight
or frozen in the tundra
and at home under desert skies.
I remember my promises
and let them guide me
when I cannot find
a better source of light.

Someone is counting on you,
I remind myself,
again and again
till I'm sure I won't forget.
I am not burdened or afraid but certain.
I can only follow through.

I do not have to win a war.
But I must be prepared
to face the battle.
In all of the moments
I think it's not possible,
I find that it is after all.

The Power of Words

My grandmother once told me
that my words had power,
that I should wield them well.
I think that's why I write.
There is power in words,
power for building
and destroying.
For hurting
and for healing.
When I want to feel powerful,
I sing out my words,
or I press them to paper
well enough to turn them real.
But here, I see things differently.
The world needs my power,
and all I have are these words.
The trees are too towering,
the skies too sweeping,
the soils too sinking,
and the lands too reaching.
The world needs my power
To fight enough to rescue it.
Yet I fear my words
and all their power
will not be powerful enough.
I find myself whispering
to my grandmother's memory.
"Nana, let my words have power,
and let it be enough."

No One Listening

I shout myself hoarse
off into the wind,
until my throat is raw
and stinging with salt.
And then still.
I lean over the sides
of the world, and I call.
My hair flying wild
all around me.
The air cooling fast
as the sun slowly falls.

"Do something!
Do something!
Do something!"

I give up my whole voice,
though no one is listening.
Until I take my words back
and promise to find them
a place where they
can be heard and heeded.

Big Corporate

This is bigger
than the workers
who gather
on the ground.
More than
the silhouette
lit by the rising sun.
And I know
it isn't people
who we all have to blame.
It's the business
with its trademark,
a trillion-dollar idea.

And until there is *action*
signed on a dotted line,
it doesn't matter
who I'm convincing.

Not unless they
can persuade someone
to stop the problem
at its source.

Compilation

So I compile all my poems
into ways they make sense.
Bunching places together
and ideas into groups.

Ruthlessly, I tear through paper pages
until only the truth earns its ink.

My poems are a battle cry,
carried over the winds.
I shout them out loud
and call myself a soldier.
I wield my words high up in the air,
and I let them lead the charge.

I raise my voice to the rooftops of
the city's tallest towers,
to the radio broadcast
and the television airwaves
and to anyone, anywhere
who might hear a thing.

Block Letters

IN ANGRY BLOCK LETTERS,
I STAND UP AND DEMAND
THAT SOMETHING CHANGES
BEFORE THE TIME'S GONE.
I HEAR THE FIRST RUMBLE
OF WHAT COULD BE A WAR,
AND I DO NOT STOP MARCHING
TOWARDS THE GREAT BATTLE.
IN ANGRY BLOCK LETTERS,
I CAN NO LONGER STAY SILENT
WHILE THE WORLD WHERE I LIVE
CRUMBLES ALL AROUND ME.
SO IN ANGRY BLOCK LETTERS,
I CALL OUT FOR HELP.
I AM A WOMAN
WHO WILL NOT
QUIET DOWN.
LIKE THE LIONS
ROAMING HERE:
HEAR.
ME.
ROAR.

Profound Yet Preventable

The impact of the Anthropocene
is profound yet preventable.
That's the great tragedy of it all.

We humans have made this
by treating the world for the taking.
And now we must suffer the price.

Profound yet preventable.

Which is to say, there's still time
for making enough of a difference
to at least slow the shift,
to find a couple more years
of good living for humankind
before it all turns,
races beyond our reach.

The cost of innovation
might be human salvation.
If we don't act now, fast,
then it's for certain.
And all I can ask
is the one thing I wonder:
what do you think
of your Anthropocene now?

The Papers

I approach all the papers
and the newscasters at five.
I try to use my voice
until it disappears,
but no matter how loud
I am shouting,
no matter who
I call out to,
no one seems to hear me.
It's as though I am trapped,
an animal in a zoo
barricaded in glass.

The people can see
that my mouth is moving,
but they cannot hear
the words that I give them
as anything other
than just muffled noise.

The papers aren't interested.
The radios don't care.
And the television shows
clear their programming
for the next plastic invention
that's advertising at prime time.

Plastered

When no one else will listen,
I turn to the streets
and find my voice
where it can't be silenced.

I take to the web and spin out like a spider.

I turn to libraries for printing posters
to pin onto streetlamps and notice boards
at the milk bar on the corner.

In the deafening city,
my voice falls on deaf ears,
lost in the sound of noise blaring, never sleeping.

I do not give up.
Plastered to every space fit for a message,
a call for help finds an audience.

In the people.
And not in the powers
that would tell them
what they should do
and think instead.

Traction

Slowly, unbelievably,
my words start to gain traction.

"I hear you. I hear you," the people begin to tell me.

Whispers of my poems drift along the street.
Replace the trademark flash of neon signs.

In the buzz of city noise,
I find a small piece of clarity
as I realise we're not alone.
Not any of us or our battles.

The people do care after all.
And now? They hear me cry.

Protests

Soon, the community launches
fast into action and takes
to the streets, a picket line.
Mass protests seize the city.
Hundreds of people gather
to demand a change now.

I finally feel something shift all around me,
when I look and see the busy street fade.

In the midst of the protests,
I discover my power.
I lead an army of us
to riling up hope.

With nothing in common
but a wish for tomorrow,
we stand tall as the towers.

And NO. We will not back down.

A Chorus

I said I would write
a song for the earth.
But now it rises
to an echoing chorus.

My voice gets lost
among all the others.
My words fly free
and find new speakers.

I said I would write
a song for the earth.
and now I stand back,
at the edge of the street,
my back leaning against
an office window
as the people charge past
and they never look back.

I said I would write
a song for the earth,
and now I am quiet
as I listen to it
sing.

Without Choices

Soon enough, the powers that be
are left without choices
but to sit up and to listen.

The louder our collective voices become.

At last, the news reports
that thousands of people
gather peacefully
in the streets
for climate action.

The corporations close ranks
and office doors.
The governments must acknowledge
the languages we speak,
must hear the words
we just won't give up on.

The powers that be
are left without choices
but to notice their impact
and to *hear* us *call.*

One Step at a Time

One step at a time, change begins.
Small projects start to launch for the better.

The process is slow,
often painstaking
as I swear we are building
from the ground up.

One step at a time, little by little,
I think I see a shift in thinking.

All this time, the climate has been changing.
Finally, I think the cities might too.

For the World Beyond

For the forest, we chase bans
to stop big business from felling the trees
and guard the lands that catch alight.
We will go where it's green
and make it greener still
with reforestation projects
designed to capture carbon
and make the air fit for breathing well again.

For the desert, we want aid
to help with the drought.
And water enough for food and for drink.
We chase climate protection
as the desert heat rises
and a plan for the sandstorms
and all their violence.
We will go to the deserts and march over the dunes
and bring resources plenty, fit for sharing.

For the ocean, we call out
for an effort to clean,
until the crashing waves are only water.
We want laws against
dumping of plastics and oils,
even in territories that don't belong
to any one country alone.
We demand a plan against acidification,
something that protects
the marine life we've let down.

In the Arctic, we demand
a new roster of scientists
to track the transition
to a much warmer world.
We want no more
fracking or drilling or mining

that only damages the permafrost worse.
We demand a close watch
on the tundra's evolution
as a signal for the world as we know it.

For the savannah, we wish
for funding and support
to keep the grasslands
from vanishing, gone.
We want agriculture
that relies on the locals
and forgets over-tilling
and pesticide poisons.
We demand a fresh focus
on the animal species
who call the prairies their home.

Unite for Change

With the last of my words,
I ask the world to listen
and to understand the need
to unite for change we choose.
It is not enough only to wait
for the climate to change around us.

We are active citizens in a world we owe our lives to.

Environmental justice
acknowledges crimes
committed against
the sorry earth
and what we can do
to change the status quo.

Me and the people,
we charge to the courts
and demand justice
for all the years
when everything
went wrong.

For the Cause

Then we are an army
of thousands for the cause
who know there's no such thing
as a quick, simple fix
and who carry on fighting anyway.
Together, we believe
that words are powerful,
but we know action
matters much more.

We do not rest
when corporations
and government officials
put their words to paper,
not until we see
a targeted impact
travel far across the world.

We march on.
For weeks, months, and years.

And we call for the change
that must not quit quickly,
that we all make each day
on behalf of the next.

A Song for the Earth

I said I would write
a song for the earth,
so I did, and now
you have found it.

Believe in the planet
and the power of your voice.
Do not fall silent when you can shout.
Do not wait for action when you can create it.

They took all my poems,
and they put them to paper,
and they called it a book
that might just
make a difference.

All of this, so long as you
remember the tune,
find the melody,
and sing it out
at the top of your lungs.

Dear reader,
    it's up to you now.
        This is a song for the earth.

Help the Cause

Like January, you can help create a greener future for our planet.

- Take steps to improve sustainability in your day-to-day life. Conserve water and energy. Replace single-use plastics with reusable alternatives. Plant a sustainable garden.
- Join an environmental organisation or citizen science program in your community. Help plant trees, clean beaches, and participate in other restorative projects.
- Follow climate scientists and educators. Expand your knowledge. Share this book with your family and friends, and start new conversations about environmental issues.
- Speak up on climate. Reach out to your local government representatives to demand better climate policies. Write your own poems. Remember, your voice has power!

Learn, Donate, or Volunteer

If you'd like to learn more, volunteer your time, or make a donation towards climate causes, try connecting with these channels.

- 350.org
- Grist
- Greenpeace
- Rainforest Trust
- The Ocean Foundation
- The Nature Conservancy
- World Wildlife Fund
- United Nations Environment Program
- Antarctic and Southern Ocean Coalition

Acknowledgements

As exciting as it is to finally be sharing *A Song for the Earth* with the world, this story wouldn't have been possible without a great number of helpers. Thank you, first and foremost, to my mum, who believed in this book before I did. Mum not only encouraged (*read* bullied) me to chase this dream. She made it possible, with regular rereads, concept sketches, and unparalleled enthusiasm. I hope get to be as cool as her one day. Another thank you to my dog and two cats – Daisy, Pixie, and Minerva. Without you lot, this book probably would have been published much sooner, but I wouldn't have it any other way. Additionally, I'd like to thank everyone who has ever helped me to become a better writer. From the professors who taught me at university to the agents and editors who offered kind, supportive, and morale-boosting feedback on the verse novel they couldn't place – thank you. To my friends, family, and social media community, who have supported my writing so far. I acknowledge the traditional custodians of beautiful lands where I live, write, and dream. Finally, to the scientists, advocates, and organisations doing good for climate causes. Thank you for all you do to make journeys like January's possible. A song for the earth is a wonderful thing when all of us sing it together.

About the Author

Shannon Jade is a writer and environmental science who believes in the power of storytelling to change the world. She is the author of Seashells for Stories, Way Back When, Rainbow, and more and has worked on books for several major publishers, including Rebel Girls and Wiley. Today, Shannon mostly writes adult fiction and poetry projects with a hopeful environmental focus, aiming to make the world a better, greener, and kinder place.

References

[1] Smith, C., Baker, J. C. A., & Spracklen, D. V. (2023). 'Tropical deforestation causes large reductions in observed precipitation,' *Nature*, vol. 615, pp. 270-275. https://doi.org/10.1038/s41586-022-05690-1.

[2] Mikkola, H. (2021). Ecosystem and biodiversity of Amazonia. Books on Demand.

[3] Fassoni-Andrade, A. C, Fleischmann, A. S., Papa, F., Paiva, R. C. D., Wongchuig, S., Melack, J. M., Moreira, A. A., Paris, A., Ruhoff, A., Barbosa, C., Maciel, D. A., Novo, E., Durand, F., Frappart, F., Aires, F., Abrahão, G. M., Ferreira-Ferreira, J., Espinoza, J. C., Laipelt, L., Costa, M. H., Espinoza-Villar, R., Calmant, S., & Pellet, V. (2021). 'Amazon hydrology from space: Scientific advances and future challenges,' *Reviews of Geophysics*, vol. 59, no. 4. https://doi.org/10.1029/2020RG000728.

[4] Youngflesh, C., Saracco, J. F., Siegel, R. B., & Tingley, M. W. (2022). 'Abiotic conditions shape spatial and temporal morphological variation in North American birds,' *Nature Ecology & Evolution*, vol. 6, pp. 1860-1870. https://doi.org/10.1038/s41559-022-01893-x.

[5] Boulton, C. A., Lenton, T. M., & Boers, N. (2022). 'Pronounced loss of Amazon rainforest resilience since the early 2000s,' *Nature Climate Change*, vol. 12, pp. 271-278. https://doi.org/10.1038/s41558-022-01287-8.

[6] Gorgens, E. B., Motta, A. Z., Assis, M., Nunes, M. H., Jackson, T., Coomes, D., Rosette, J., Aragão, L. E. O. C., Omette, J. P. (2019). 'The giant trees of the Amazon basin,' *Frontiers in Ecology and the Environment*, vol. 17, no. 7, pp. 373-374. https://doi.org/10.1002/fee.2085.

[7] Dos Santos, K. M. & Campos, T. V. O. (2005). 'Amazon rainforest: Biodiversity and biopiracy,' *BMJ*, vol. 13. https://doi.org/10.1136/sbmj.0510386.

[8] World Wildlife Fund (n.d.). Inside the Amazon. https://wwf.panda.org/discover/knowledge_hub/where_we_work/amazon/about_the_amazon/.

[9] World Wildlife Fund (n.d.). The Amazon. https://www.wwf.org.uk/where-we-work/amazon.

[10] Ogasa N. (2023). The Amazon is in trouble. Here's why – and why it matters, Science News Explores. https://www.snexplores.org/article/why-amazon-rainforest-in-trouble-climate-deforestation.

[11] Liu, Y. & Xue, Y. (2020). 'Expansion of the Sahara Desert and shrinking of frozen land of the Arctic', Sci Rep, vol. 10, https://doi.org/10.1038/s41598-020-61085-0.

[12] Britannica (n.d.). Drainage of the Sahara, https://www.britannica.com/place/Sahara-desert-Africa/Drainage.

[13] Yu, H., Tan, Q., Zhou, L., Zhou, Y., Bian, H., Chin, M., Ruder, C. L., Levy, R. C., Pradhan, Y., Shi, Y., Song, Q., Zhang, Z., Colarco, P. R., Kim, D., Remer, L. A., Yuan, T., Mayol-Bracero, O. & Holben, B. N. (2021). 'Observation and modelling of the historic "Godzilla" African dust intrusion into the Caribbean Basin and the southern US in June 2020', *Atmospheric Chemistry and Physics*, vol. 21, no. 16, pp.12359-12383. https://doi.org/10.5194/acp-21-12359-2021.

[14] National Oceanic and Atmospheric Administration (2024)., How much water is in the ocean?. https://oceanservice.noaa.gov/facts/oceanwater.html.

[15] Fava, M. (2022). How much of the ocean has been explored?, UNESCO. https://oceanliteracy.unesco.org/ocean-exploration/.

[16] United Nations Regional Information Centre for Western Europe (2023). Global warming: 90% of emissions heat absorbed by the ocean, https://unric.org/en/global-warming-90-of-emissions-heat-absorbed-by-the-ocean/.

[17] OCEANA (n.d.). Effects of climate change on the oceans. https://usa.oceana.org/our-work-climate-energy-climate-change-learn-act-impacts-of-climate-change-on-the-oceans/.

[18] The Ocean Cleanup (2018). Great Pacific Garbage Patch growing rapidly, study shows. https://theoceancleanup.com/press/press-releases/great- pacific-garbage-patch-growing-rapidly-study-shows/.

[19] Lebreton, L., Slat, B., Ferrari, F., Sainte-Rose, B., Aitken, J., Marthouse, R., Hajbane, S., Cunsolo, S., Schwarz, A., Levivier, A., Noble, K., Debeljak, P., Maral, H., Schoeneich-Argent, R., Brambini, R. & Reisser, J. (2018). 'Evidence that the Great Pacific Garbage Patch is rapidly accumulating plastic,' *Scientific Reports*, vol. 8. https://doi.org/10.1038/s41598-018-22939-w.

[20] Dalberg & The University of Newcastle, Australia (2019). No plastic in nature: Assessing plastic ingestion from nature to people. https://assets.wwf.org.au/image/upload/v1/website-media/resources/pub-no-plastic-in-nature-assessing-plastic-ingestion-from-nature-to-people-jun19?.

[21] National Geographic (n.d.). Great Pacific Garbage Patch. https://education.nationalgeographic.org/resource/great-pacific-garbage-patch/.

[22] World Wildlife Fund Australia (2021). The lifecycle of plastics. https://wwf.org.au/blogs/the-lifecycle-of-plastics/.

[23] Great Lakes Commission (n.d.). About the Lakes. https://www.glc.org/lakes/.

[24] Dobrijevic, D. & Waldeck, S. (2023). Northern lights (aurora borealis): What they are & how to see them, Space.com, https://www.space.com/15139-northern-lights-auroras-earth-facts-sdcmp.html.

[25] Nikel, D. (2023). Living on Svalbard: Everything you need to know, Life in Norway. https://www.lifeinnorway.net/living-on-svalbard/.

[26] Kulturhuset stadsteatern (n.d.). https://kulturhusetstadsteatern.se/english.

[27] Watts, J. (2019). Welcome to the fastest heating place on Earth, The Guardian, https://www.theguardian.com/environment/ng-interactive/2019/jul/01/its-getting-warmer-wetter-wilder-the-arctic-town-heating-faster-than-anywhere.

[28] United States Environmental Protection Agency (2023). Climate change indicators: ice sheets. https://www.epa.gov/climate-indicators/climate-change-indicators-ice-sheets.

[29] Rantanen, M., Karpechko, A. Y., Lipponen, A., Nordling, K., Hyva◇rinen, O., Ruosteenoja, K., Vihma, T. & Laaksonen, A. (2022). 'The Arctic has warmed nearly four times faster than the globe since 1979,' Communications Earth & Environment, vol. 3. https://doi.org/10.1038/s43247-022- 00498-3.

[30] Zhang, X., Tang, H., Zhang, J., Walsh, J. E., Roesler, E. L., Hillman, B., Ballinger, T. M. & Weijer, W. (2023). 'Arctic cyclones have become more intense and longer-lived over the past seven decades,' Communications Earth & Environment, vol. 4. https://doi.org/10.1038/s43247-023-01003-0.

[31] Center for Biological Diversity (n.d.). Polar Bear, https://www.biological-diversity.org/species/mammals/polar_bear/.

[32] Rawlence, B. (2022). 'The treeline is out of control': How the climate crisis is turning the Arctic green, The Guardian, https://www.theguardian.com/news/2022/jan/20/norway-arctic-circle-trees-sami-reindeer-global-heating.

[33] Lo, J. (2022). Destruction of Brazil's Cerrado savanna soars for third year in a row, Climate Home News, https://www.climatechangenews.com/2022/12/15/destruction-of-brazils-cerrado-savanna-soars-for-third-year-in-a-row/.

[34] National Park Service (n.d.). Tallgrass prairie. https://www.nps.gov/tapr/learn/nature/a-complex-prairie-ecosystem.htm.

[35] World Wildlife Fund (n.d.). Global grasslands and savannahs initiative, https://wwf.panda.org/discover/our_focus/food_practice/grasslands_and_savannahs/.

www.ingramcontent.com/pod-product-compliance
Lightning Source LLC
Chambersburg PA
CBHW011734020426
42333CB00024B/2888